Mindful Mom

HOW TO CREATE THE BEST TIME OF YOUR LIFE

Anna Meiwes

EMPOWERING
INSPIRATIONS
FOR
AWESOME
MOMS

To order additional copies of this book, contact:
Xlibris
844-714-8691
www.Xlibris.com
Orders@Xlibris.com

ISBN: Softcover   978-1-6641-5669-2
        Hardcover   978-1-6641-5670-8
        EBook   978-1-6641-5668-5

Print information available on the last page

Rev. date: 03/26/2021

Contents

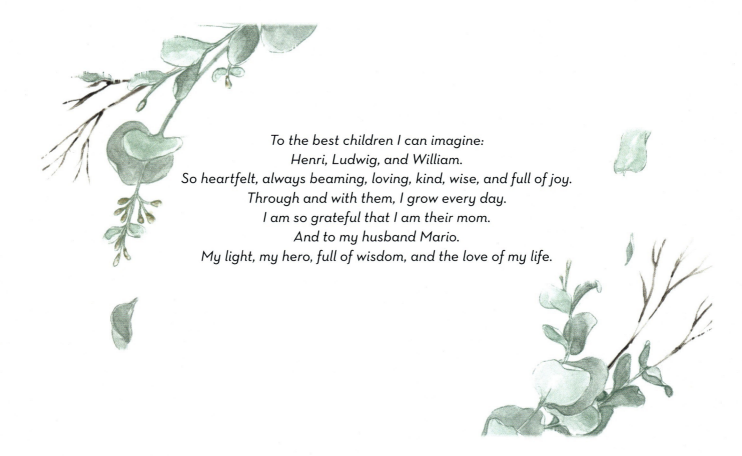

To the best children I can imagine:
Henri, Ludwig, and William.
So heartfelt, always beaming, loving, kind, wise, and full of joy.
Through and with them, I grow every day.
I am so grateful that I am their mom.
And to my husband Mario.
My light, my hero, full of wisdom, and the love of my life.

Introduction

Imagine experiencing blessings every day with your children: moments of fulfillment, laughter, creativity; clowning around and having fun; feeling so filled with love and so grateful for having the best children you can imagine; being full of energy *and* still being able to accomplish all your daily duties in a way to be satisfied and content.

That is possible for every parent and for you!

This is a book for all moms who are "fighting" to be the best mom for their little miracles every day, trying to combine job, household duties, cooking, laundry, playing with the kids, taking care of all appointments, other family members, friends, neighborhood, church duties, etc., as well as moms who are trying to stay healthy, patient, relaxed, and serene. In fact, most parents experience their parenthood, livelihood, and ordinary life as exhausting and overwhelming. They are stressed out, lacking proper sleep, lacking proper healthy food, and most of all, lacking happiness. They feel too tired to enjoy life with their children and to follow the values that are most important to them. On top of that, they feel guilty for not having done enough for the most important in life: their little treasures, their children.

This book shows simple ways to bring more flow into your parenting by explaining how to create new habits to take care of yourself, recharge yourself, and replenish yourself.

Ask yourself: How do you want to be as a mom—stressed out, always rushing, exhausted, never having time to enjoy life and your loved ones, afterward feeling guilty although you gave your best all day long and worked so hard, yet still there is this feeling of not having done enough? With this frustrated feeling, most mothers and fathers fall asleep or cannot fall asleep and are pondering what to do or to change, getting nowhere. Every idea is stopped by the thought "There isn't enough time" or "I can't change the circumstances," and with a depressed feeling, you experience poor sleep and wake up in a bad mood. The same vicious circle of rushing, running, fighting, feeling bad and not good enough starts all over again day after day. This is not your fault. Simply, how to take care of ourselves as parents is not taught in strategies for parenting.

I strongly believe that self-care, which is a part of self-love, is the key for holistic health and successful parenting in terms of enjoyment and happiness. Imagine if you would take care of yourself on a regular basis.

What does that mean, being a mom/dad? You enjoy your children because you are energized, balanced, and lighthearted.

What does that mean for your work? You are productive because you feel so energized, healthy, fit, and strong. You have better concentration and overflowing creativity, which may even get you a promotion or a better job in the long run.

What does that mean for your relationships? You are a better listener because you are balanced, relaxed, and happy. You can be more emphatic. You don't feel defensive with others and always see the best in others.

What does that mean for your health? You have a strong immune system, and you rarely become sick.

The best of self-care is: You are laughing more. You live the life that is successful on your own terms. You fall asleep with a feeling of deep peace to be nothing but positive. You lived the day in your full presence, soaking in your children, enjoying your work, and being mindful in all your interactions with others. You feel connected with others and yourself. You respond from insight instead of reacting from the ego. You just have that wonderful feeling that you live a purposeful life.

How blessed would you feel after such a great day?

In this book, you will get insights on how to get there. By using science-proven facts about mindfulness and holistic health, backed up by research combined with the science of happiness, you will get inspirations in the following story.

The story of Mindful Mom and her wonderful children is my own journey with my family. My intention is to reach your mind and your heart and to create a new mind and heart set for a true change in your experience as a parent. You can see the book as an inspiration buffet, from which you can simply pick the most resonating ideas and try them. My intention is not to make you believe that you need to be perfect as a mother. Resist the idea of trying to accomplish every strategy at once. Keep in mind, even though Mindful Mom is doing a lot for her happiness and livir U1 .i life with her children every day, it d yo nean she is perfect! Nobody is! There still moments when she loses her temper, is impatient, overwhelmed, and stressed out. Those moments are worthy to practice compassion, forgiveness, and mindfulness for yourself and grow from there. For me, being a mom is the best, most beautiful, at the same time, challenging, emotional, and the most important thing to experience in life.

I feel blessed that you have chosen to read this, that I can be a part of your journey as a mom. If it is just one thought, idea, inspiration that impacts your and your children's life in a positive way, then this book is purposeful.

If you are reading this, it means you are willing to change something. You took action for your growth. It is already proven that you are a good parent because you make efforts. Your children and your family life are so important to you that you took action to buy and read this book. Thank yourself!

As a main tool and strategy, you will find mindfulness in different ways. Every story, poem, and advice are colored with benefits from a mindful behavior and mindset toward others, yourself, and your precious child(-ren).

It would me make happy if you can enjoy this journey and let yourself be touched by reading my story, becoming inspired to open your heart for a transformation toward enjoying parenting, increasing your holistic health and your personal happiness. Starting with ourselves makes the world a better place.

You are where you are supposed to be. Reading this book can be a big step toward a meaningful and powerful life as a parent and a human being.

3

Mindfulness is an awareness to the present moment; bringing your attention from the past and the future to the right here, right now, and living the present moment fully; being aware of your feelings, thoughts, and body as a part of yourself without judging anything.

Mindfulness is experiencing yourself, others, and your environment with your full presence, compassion, and heartfulness.

Through letting go of all judgments about yourself and others, you create strength, joy, and inner peace. It helps you switch from an autopilot state to a state of truly living. It's about being there as if it's the first time you see the other one (for example, your child) and learning to appreciate everything that you experience.

—Mindful Mom

 You are enough and worthy.
You are a good mom.

To live is the rarest thing in the world. Most people exist, that's all.

—*Oscar Wilde*

Connecting

How often do you connect with your child?

Do you think it has been a while?

It is time to reflect on that

Which doesn't mean you are "bad"

It's just so good to evaluate from time to time

And decide which type of parenting is mine

Which feels most right - most fulfilled for me

Which makes me feel free

Connecting can be in so many ways

A talk, a smile, a touch on the child's face

A mindful moment between you two

You will feel the inner truth

Of life and feeling alive

By giving yourself daily time

For mindfulness between you and your loved one

Stop yourself from rushing and running

Daily business, duties, and all that needs to be done

Just hold on and be aware of your treasure in front

This little blessing running around you

So joyful, so peaceful, and without any adult's "truths"

Avoid regrets, didn't have enough time to enjoy your kids

Do it right now and do everything that fits

Everyday moments of laughter and stillness between you and your children

You will discover a beautiful bliss that you don't even know

Mindful Connecting: Being totally present (mindful) in the sharing of the moment/experience with your child; no judging, total openness for your child's and your needs (intentions, thoughts, feelings); seeing your child like the first time; letting go of everything else and being fully aware of yourself and your child.

Respond to any situation with the question in mind: What action would be the most serving here?

You are enough and worthy.

You are enough and worthy.
You are a good mom.

Beliefs You Give Your Children

Lorelei asks Mindful Mom: How do you deal with it when your children are fighting with each other?

Mindful Mom: I am overly cautious how to respond because I don't want my children to feel they are not good enough or bad, no matter what they did.

An example from yesterday:

Henri: Mom, Ludwig pulled me and squeezed my arm.

Mindful Mom: Ludwig, come here, please. What happened?

Ludwig: I was angry that Henri didn't give me the little toy horse.

Mindful Mom: It's okay when you have "negative" feelings or emotions, everybody does, but we can deal with it without hurting others. I know you don't want to hurt Henri. He is your best friend. If you feel angry, you can either tell him "I feel angry" or you go to your cuddling monster Charly and squeeze him until your anger can "flow through you." You could do shadow-boxing or clapping. Which possibility would you like to try out?

Ludwig: I'll go and fetch Charly.

Mindful Mom: What did we learn from this? There are many possibilities to deal with "negative" emotions without hurting someone. And when you feel relieved again, you try to find something else to play with and distract yourself with.

Mindful Mom: You see, if I would punish Ludwig, his belief would be "I am not okay," even beliefs like "I am not good enough," "Mom doesn't like me." Every time we experience challenging behavior with our children, we can ask ourselves,

Which belief will stick after our conversation or consequence?

Children tend to connect the punishment with their own personality at least until eleven years old. They feel bad about themselves and learn unhealthy beliefs, which may stick until adolescence.

You are enough and worthy

What Is Family About?

How wonderful family can be

All this warmth and heartfulness you can feel

Big and little moments of fulfillment

Tears and laughter, anger, and again being friends

Sharing, giving, taking, and loving

Snapshot the little moments of this wonderful being

Making the best of everything:

Even with illness or chores - you can sing

Not taking personally anything that goes wrong

With hard feelings – you don't feel alone

Children are good examples of that

They are never resentful or feel a threat

We can learn from them in that manner

Already forgotten and forgiven and nonjudging behavior

Just letting go of this negative feeling

Like your little loved ones almost always beaming

Sharing adventures, it doesn't matter if it costs anything

No matter if it is a stone, an acorn, or a ring

For children, everything that creates fun is equally special

The adults think we need to go on vacation

But ordinary things like going for a walk

Can turn into the best adventure and talk

By being mindful in every moment

Your inner child will awake instead of feeling homeless

The little ones feel it and enjoy being present with you

Those are the best moments and this is the whole truth

Mini-Mindfulness

Henri: Mom, can you tell me a story?

Mindful Mom: What kind of story do you want me to tell you?

Henri: I don't know, whatever comes to your mind.

Without thinking about it, Mindful Mom starts with the story.

Mindful Mom: There was a princess named Isabel. She was always listening to her inner voice, to her feelings, before she did anything. At the breakfast table, the queen said, "Eat your cereal."

Isabel said, "But without milk."

The queen asked, "Why?"

"It just feels right,", said Isabel.

In the afternoon, Isabel decided to go for a walk into the woods. As always, she trusted her feelings where to go. After a while, she met a bear and asked him, "You won't do anything to me, will you?"

The bear answered, "No, but I am just so hungry, and I don't know where to go to search for food."

Isabel said, "Okay. I will help you with a mini-mindful exercise. Sit down with me and watch me. Put your thumbs to your forefingers and clench them softly while you breathe in.

Mindful Mom: Henri, come, do it with me like Isabel and the bear. Hold on for a while and let go of the pressure and the breath. Then connect your thumbs with the middle fingers and again press softly and breathe in, hold, and breathe out and let the fingers relax. We go on with the ring finger and then with the small finger. And then backward.

Isabel asked, "How does that feel to you, bear?"

The bear said, "Oh, I feel so good, and even my hunger isn't that bad anymore. Also, there is a feeling that I could find some food at the river. Would you like to accompany me?"

At the river, the bear was able to find a lot of fish he could eat, and Isabel was happy to see him so happy. Even happier was she that her *mini-mindfulness* helped the bear. So she said goodbye and went back home, thinking, "That was the reason I had the intuition to go into the woods, to help the bear and show him how he can relax and listen to his inner voice."

Mindful Mom: And in this way, you can hear your own inner impulses better, your intuition, Henri. Through taking just a few minutes to calm down and pay attention to your breath.

You are enough and worthy.

My First Miracle

Oh, Henri,

How wonderful was this evening with you?

So many moments I thought this is the whole truth!

How can a human being be so amazing?

Lightening from the inside and gazing

All around at what brings joy to him

In everything, he sees a miracle - glimpse

Of a blessing, beauty, and perfection

In his eyes, you see his heart's reaction

Moment by moment just enjoying time together

This experience will be in our hearts forever

At the YMCA tae kwon do and exercise

We went to a parlor for ice cream and french fries

I was soaking in the awesomeness of this child

So smart, handsome, and so, so bright

I still remember I was pregnant with you almost six years ago

Then a great year after year in a row

My baby was sleeping on my chest

And now he seems to be almost out of our nest

I can't believe how time flies by

That's why it's so important to enjoy

Special and daily moments with each other

We won't always have so much time as son and mother

I am so grateful that I am your mom

You are an incredibly special human being with your inner warmth

- Henri, you are amazing. Mom will always love you.

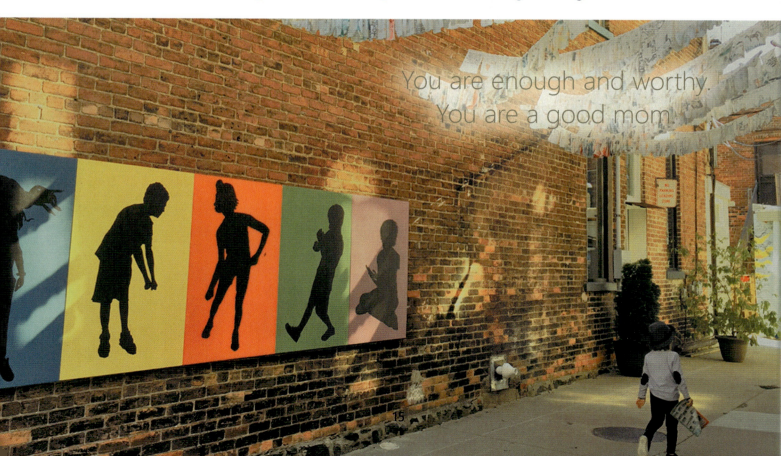

You are enough and worthy.
You are a good mom

The teeth-brushing song

Mindful Mom: Come on, my best ones, it's time for brushing your teeth.

Henri and Ludwig: No-o, we don't want to!

Mindful Mom: Come on, we'll sing our song:

Bacteria, bacteria, we're brushing all away

Bacteria, bacteria, you will be soon afraid

Bacteria say, "no, no, no!"

Yes, we are brushing all away, and the dentist says, "Great!"

Henri and Ludwig like to brush their teeth three times a day.

Don't Beat Up On Yourself

Every moment is a new one

Focus on the present moment and stop going on and on

Always running away from everything that feels "bad"

Anger, anxiety, bad feelings, and threats

Against yourself not being good enough as a mom

Don't forget - you always do the best you can

In every given moment, it is possible

To be the best version of yourself

Embrace the unwanted and don't push it away

As you accept all the "dark parts" inside you; they won't stay

Without dark, there is no light

You do one thing imperfectly but also thousands right

You give so much every day to your loved ones

Don't forget to give to yourself as well

Replenish body, mind, and soul

That makes a deep difference and plays a huge role

How resiliently you can deal with daily challenges

So much better when mind and soul are fresh

Find a few minutes as often as you can

Throughout the day and create a nice moment for yourself

17

Strengthen Self-Awareness

Mindful Mom: Tell me something you are proud of today, something you did or accomplished or how you reacted or treated another.

Henri: I am proud that I played today with Ludwig and that we shared.

Ludwig: I am grateful for my toys and that Mommy is always so cuddling.

Ludwig doesn't really understand the difference between the gratitude exercise and the self-awareness exercise. But that doesn't matter. The most important is that he is a part of our ritual and has fun and falls asleep with a good feeling.

Mindful Mom: I am proud of you both that you played so well with each other. And I am proud of myself that I could go to the gym and enjoy a Zumba class while being pregnant with your brother William.

You Are A Goddess

Cleaning, cooking, laundry, teeth-brushing

Everything you do for your loved ones is astonishing

Playing, organizing, soothing, and so much more

Every day's duties in- and outside your door

We tend to take it for granted

But you should know - it is not!

You are amazing - a true goddess

Doing everything for your loved ones and for yourself no less

Every day you nourish their bodies and souls

With love and kindness and patience in turn

Every time you show them unconditional love

Their souls flourish more and more

Like a goddess, you accomplish one thousand things at the same time

*Even if exhausted, tired, overwhelmed, you are always there
for them*

Be aware of your amazing beingness

Always embracing, kissing, listening upon your chest

The next time you do the chores

Think "I am a goddess" - I really am and roar

Uplift and say "thank you" to yourself as often as you can

Stop running and be mindful every now and then

Reflect on how many big and little things you did today

It is time to do the same for yourself

Because only a healthy mom can continue to give

Only a happy mom can be the best parent they need

You may have time for yourself

You deserve it - don't forget it!

Anna Meiwes

You are enough and worthy.
You are a good mom.

Happiness diary

Henri: Mom, what are you doing?

Mindful Mom: I am writing in my happiness book about our day today. It made me feel so happy to see you playing in the snow and laughing, to watch you with your brother Ludwig playing together and having fun; the abundance of time we have together and that I had time to read a book while you were playing, that I cooked a fresh soup for us to enjoy after being outside in the cold, and the moment as your dad danced with me in the kitchen to the song "Always Remember Us This Way" (Lady Gaga).

Henri: That sounds like our gratitude diary.

Mindful Mom: Yes, you can call it that way or *my book of appreciation* or *my happiness book*, whatever feels right and uplifting to you.

Next day:

Lorelei: Henri told me, when he was playing here, that you are writing a special diary with him and on your own. He was so amazed and beaming as he talked about it. What is it all about?

Mindful Mom: Oh, you mean our happiness diary! This is so much fun: Buy a nice notebook that delights you, one that inspires you and that you like to hold in your hand (at first, you can start just on a normal sheet of paper).

At the end of the day, ask yourself which moments made me feel happy, relaxed, fulfilled, or joyous. And you write down everything that comes to your mind. It is important that you relive that moment and feel the appreciation for around seventeen to thirty seconds on every entry. Savor it, feel gratitude and enjoyment. When you do it on a regular basis, you will notice that you fall asleep with a good feeling, which enhances the quality of your sleep, and you will wake up in a better mood. That sets up your day in a positive direction. You become more and more aware of all the good things around you.

This wonderful tool helps you focus on what good things have happened during the day, and it's immensely powerful. You can also name it *my gratitude diary* or *my book of appreciations* or *my book of blessings*, whatever resonates most with you and gives you a lighthearted feeling.

Lorelei: Is there any proof that it works?

Mindful Mom: Yes, there is a lot of research in positive psychology nowadays about the positive effect of gratitude as a resource to enhance well-being. For example, they say people that are more grateful feel happier, are healthier, and are more fulfilled. Grateful people experience less depression and anxiety. If you use this awesome resource consciously, the body produces dopamine and serotonin, "the happiness hormones." Isn't that amazing? We have this incredible and simple resource inside us for free that benefits our well-being in so many ways.

Lorelei: That sounds wonderful. I will go and get a nice journal today!

Mindful Mom: Yes, I just love it.

You know, our children are overly sensitive when it comes to knowing whether we are happy or not. Part of our role as mothers is to work on ourselves and learn how to be more joyful through self-care and practicing mindfulness. Our children notice consciously or subconsciously that you are taking care of yourself, feeling happy and serene. Also, they learn from you when you show that your mood doesn't depend on circumstances or what other people are doing or thinking. They learn that you can decide how to respond to events and that it is the meaning you attach to circumstances that is the most important. How awesome and empowering is that? That doesn't mean you shall feel guilty when there are times you don't feel happy or joyous.

When you feel "negative" emotions you can be mindful with yourself: that means you try to be aware of that feeling without judging yourself. You can also discover how you notice this feeling in your body. Is there heaviness/ pressure/ narrowness at your chest/ on your shoulders/ in your belly?

It is just an opportunity to grow in that area without trying to push it away. Practicing just to notice when you feel stuck, negative, depressed without fixing on that feeling or negative thought, just being aware of it, being mindful and compassionate with yourself in such moments. And then practicing with little tools like the gratitude journal, how to raise your energy and happiness level.

And the by-product is that you have way more fun in your daily life, you strengthen your holistic health, and you can accomplish so much more easily all the ordinary duties. Also, you will benefit in your relationships. When you are aware of your mood and raise your happiness level through self-care, you can deal with problems so much better and respond to everyone mindfully, patiently, and kindly.

So how can we grow our level of consciousness and practice self-care toward more health and happiness? By practicing mindfulness throughout the day, introducing little habits for yourself that feel good to you and energize you, like yoga, your gratitude diary; being creative; having time for yourself to do whatever you enjoy and recharge you. You may start with five minutes a day and expand from here. The result will be immediate.

The gratitude journaling is a wonderful way to start.

Research shows:
Practicing gratitude enhances overall well-being. -

Tool Gratitude Journal – Buy a nice notebook. Write down three to ten things that you are grateful for every evening or morning. If that is too much for you, do it once a week or choose one thing and write down a sentence about it. Try to be aware of your luck and feel the emotion for at least a few seconds. You will notice the difference in your well-being after a few weeks.

In this moment, there is plenty of time. In this moment, you are precisely as you should be. In this moment, there is infinite potential.

Victoria Moran

Mindful Mom's friend Lorelei: You know, I am just so sick and tired. Every evening is the same. The kids are hyperactive, not listening, and I am so tired and just yelling at them. It takes more than an hour for bed, feels like a fight, and afterward, I am so exhausted. On the top of that, I am feeling guilty. I don't know what to do.

Mindful Mom: I can feel for you. Sometimes, after a busy or exhausting day, we feel like putting the kids to bed is an exhausting hurdle. We feel tired and are not aware of that big gift and even privilege to be able to put our loved ones to bed, to be needed, to feel and share being connected with the biggest treasures in our life, being able to spend precious moments with those we love the most, in fact moments that never come back as the same. Even just being aware of that helps change your perception from "I need to" to "I may."

It helps to get a new point of view to raise your energy. If you just think about it, later, in twenty or thirty years, you will look back and will wish to get back to this point where your children were so small and craved your good-night kisses. So see the situation from that point of view, and you will immediately notice how you raise your energy and enjoy the good-night situation.

Also, you can do something to have fun with your children, for example:

- read a good-night story in a dark room with a flashlight
- let everyone continue the story in a row
- jump on the bed before or after reading
- change the set point of your nightly bed routine
- sing a song together

Start with the routines half hour earlier and notice the difference when you have more time and energy for your children to make bedtime easier.

It is worth it to be more mindful of that part of your day. If you take care of that, you can end your day so much easier and more peacefully with the feeling that you did it "right," right in terms of I was fully there when my kids listened to me as I read the story, I noticed the sparkling in their eyes, I savored their laughter and smiles, I savored singing for them, kissing them, and saying how much I love them.

Being mindful with your loved ones gives you feelings of peace and forges deeper connections. You can experience the most important fuel: **sharing real deep moments with each other**.

This evening Lorelei started a half hour earlier with the bedtime routine and tried out something new: the gratitude ritual. Everything went more smoothly, the children were amazed, and Lorelei felt at peace like never after putting her little treasures to bed.

Just Today

Just today I don't want to judge

No matter if I am eating a salad or fudge

Just today I want to forgive myself

And everything that isn't perfectly made

Just today I don't want to judge others

Just today I see all as my friendship souls

Just today I see myself as my best friend

Forgive and forget everything where I misbehaved and made mistakes

Just today I like my body, my character, and all what belongs to me

Just today, no matter what, I feel free

Just today I want to remind me that I have a choice

Every time before I raise my voice

Just today I only radiate joy and happiness

Just today I see around me only finesse

Just today I stop criticizing

Just today I start rather praising

Just today I feel like a king

Just today I feel lovable and amazing

Just today I want to frankly express my feelings

Just today, no excuses, rather clearings

Just today I will love everyone

Just today I will love myself like a caring mom

But wait, why just today??
I can choose right here and right now to live that way every day

May you live every day of your life.

—*Jonathan Swift*

Practice Good-feeling thoughts

PARENTING

I love kissing my babies all the time and cuddling them all the time. I love showing and telling them how much I love them, and I love doing it often. I love their little butts and their long hair and every detail in their face. I love seeing their excitement when they tell me about their thoughts. I like it when I am mindful in those moments and savor those glimpses of total bliss and fulfillment. I love being a mom. I love explaining to them how the body works. I like explaining to them what is healthy and what is not. I love to watch them when they play with each other and are totally caught up in their game and children's world. I love everything they wear. I like how strong they are and still needy and helpless. I love making them laugh and giggling with them. I love it when we clown around together and we create events and memories.

I feel so honored that I can be their mom. I love it when we reconcile with each other with our *peace sign* after an argument and hug and kiss each other. I love how we then appreciate the peace even more after the argument. I embrace our daily life full of laughing, harmony, and joy of life! I love how they say goodbye with kissing and hugging when I am leaving and with smiling when I return. I love doing something adventurous with my children. I like singing songs with them and about them and for them. I love dancing with them. I love calling them "my best ones" and singing about how great they are. I also appreciate the moment of stillness when we are painting, crafting, or just resting. I love that they are whispering when I am resting or meditating. How awesome is that? I love seeing them when we are around and with other people. I just think I do have the best children on earth and how blessed we are. I enjoy being in cafés with my little ones. I love enjoying life and playing with them. I am so grateful for all our journeys and road trips through America. I love running through puddles after a summer rain in front of our house. I love to discover the world through their eyes with them and so much more!

What do you like about being a mom?

Raise-Your-Energy Tool:

Pick an area of your life (job, parenting, work, hobby) or a person that/who is important to you and write down what you love about it/him/her. You will notice how grateful, blissful, and fulfilled you will feel after that little "heart exercise."

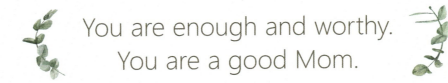

You are enough and worthy.
You are a good Mom.

Practice Good-feeling thoughts

MY JOB

I like the feeling of my passion. I like to read, to grow, and to teach all these topics. I love the flow of feeling when I am teaching my classes. I love seeing when people get an ah-ha! moment. I really like when people tell me their stories and I can inspire them. I like that they trust my knowledge as life coach and mindfulness coach. I love feeling resonance in my whole body when I say something that is really true for me. I love even the smell of my practice room. I love seeing the fire of joy and hope of the people who are listening. I love it when I see people feeling worthy and enough and motivated to "conquer the world." Oh, I just love my work! I like to draw something on the easel to explain a connection. I love asking questions and presenting all I know so the people can pick the information that feels right for them and try it out. I like my groups and all the people I meet and get to know. I appreciate everything about it.

WHAT DO *YOU* LIKE ABOUT YOUR JOB?

Our children's Mission

Lorelei: I don't get it. The first child is just like perfect. Everything works well since he is born, never a problem. Everything went smoothly. But the second child is almost the opposite of that: trying to find his place in the family, often impatient, not listening; and sometimes I just go crazy.

Mindful Mom: Every parent gets the kids they need to have. They are chosen to be their parents. Notice what exactly annoys you when your child isn't listening or is impatient.

Are you reminded of your own impatience?

What happens if you learn to accept your "weak" character trait through your child?

One function of our children is to push our "emotional buttons." The things that annoy us are unresolved things within ourselves. Be mindful of your feelings toward your children. Be aware of your feelings and thoughts about them and their behavior. Just notice without fixing. It says a lot about yourself. Everything happens for a reason. You and I and any other parent are blessed with the children we have and got exactly the children we need so we can grow as human beings.

Lorelei: Okay, I got it. But what happens then? If I notice that my daughter's messiness reminds me of my own, what can I do?

Mindful Mom: You embrace your imperfection by for example saying a mantra like:

It's okay not being perfect.

I accept myself totally.

I forgive myself for not being perfect, and I always do my best.

You just notice it without trying to change anything. Self-awareness is the first step. Try to get to a place of compassion for yourself and your child. Take one deep breath and then come back.

Appreciate the good things about your child.

When you direct your focus on the things that work well, they become more. Attention creates more energy for the things you are focused on.

Every moment is fresh beginning.

—T. S. Elliot

Anna Meiwes

You Are Enough Und Worthy.
You Are A Good Dad.

Set A
Positive Intention

When the kids are still sleeping, Mindful Mom is awake to replenish herself, to welcome her *best ones* in the new day full of positive energy, good feelings, lightheartedness, and relaxation. She would take her notebook that is at her night table and start journaling to set up a positive intention and raise her mood.

My I Ams

I am blessed.

I am heartfulness.

I am love and kindness.

I am Mindful Mom.

I am kissing and cuddling.

I am free and freedom.

I am soulfulness.

I am gratitude.

I am seeing the best in others.

I am trusting and knowing.

I am peace.

I am at ease.

I am eager to embrace the new day.

I am creative.

I am following my inner voice.

I am relaxation.

I am forgiveness.

I am good enough.

I am always doing my best.

I am mindful with myself, with others, and with my day.

I am living my own truth.

I am blessed.

I am abundance.

I am already everything I need to be happy.

I am serenity.

I am authentic.

I am worthy.

35

When her children wake up, Mindful Mom is recharged with a positive mindset and heartset. Her brain is rewired to be aware of the positive things. She can be the best version of herself and embrace all things with more ease, patience, and enjoyment. Her children feel how relaxed and happy their mom is and reflect that in their own behavior.

What a wonderful "miracle morning."

The "I Am" Tool: To set a positive intention for your day, write down ten to twenty-five characteristics that feel good to you, strengthen you, lift you up, and you resonate with, and repeat every morning. Soon you will notice a positive effect on your day.

You can also start just with one *"I am"* and grow from there, if that is easier for your schedule.

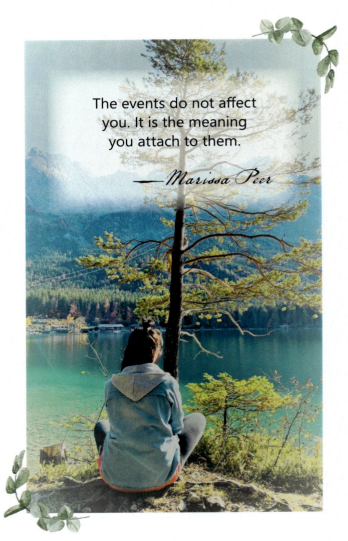

The events do not affect you. It is the meaning you attach to them.

—*Marissa Peer*

Mindfulness:
The Door To Happiness

All I can find is a blissful feeling

Encounter my thoughts and my energy is driven

A wonderful feeling of contentment that will flow into you

Mindfulness benefits are around you through and through

It gives you peace

This feeling of a huge release

Letting go of everything that isn't important

Social media, TV, work, duties, and tasks, on and on

What is really important to me?

What gives me the feeling to be free?

To live from the insight in my own terms of happiness

You will discover unrest less and less

Take a few deep breaths right now

You will feel an impulse in turn

At least once a day allow yourself to take time

For daydreaming about your dreams for a while

About the things that are really touching your inner core

Your main goals for your life – try something new more and more

Let them come and feel the accomplishment of them

Feel and imagine your goals like you would sleep in 'REM'

Relaxed and detached from everything

A healing state of being is this happiness - glimpse

Nobody

can wrong you

Mindful Dad, shouting: You never listen to me. I told you this so many times, and you always do it the other way, and afterward, you are complaining about it.

Mindful Mom, yelling back: Can you just be kinder and say that in another way? How can you be so disrespectful? You are treating me like a nobody.

After a few loud arguments between them, Mindful Mom goes out of the room, still feeling mad and frustrated. While preparing herself for a shower, still with a lot of anger in her being, a thought occurs to her: If I would not take the reproach in a personal way about myself, it wouldn't touch me anyways. He just pushed my buttons. So I am unsatisfied, meaning, I would like to grow there. This bothers me about myself.

Suddenly, the anger just flew away. And now she was totally clear to ask her brain about a strategy: how she could grow in that area. Immediately, an idea came to her mind. The topic they had an argument was working with her computer and saving properly some data. Now she has the thought, *To remember these steps, I will write it down in a notebook.*

After that enlightening moment, it became so easy to reconnect with her significant other in a loving and forgiving way.

Mindful Mom reminds herself that being mindful with your feelings and thoughts can have a huge impact for all your relationships.

Mindfulness Tool: Observer Mind

Every time you feel defended or you judge another person, notice what feelings arise. Where and how does it feel in your body? Try to describe/name it without judging. To create distance from your ego's side, you can use a sentence like "This is how [anger/frustration, etc.] feels like." By doing that, you step back and create space for a connection, responding instead of fearful or defensive reacting.

Ask yourself: Do I think about me that way? Are there parts that are triggered through him/her that I don't like about myself? Were there situations I behaved the same way that I am judging now?

When I was five years old, my mother always told me that happiness is the key to life. When I went to school, they asked me what I wanted to be when I grew up. I wrote down "happy." They told me I didn't understand the assignment, and I told them they didn't understand life.

—John Lennon

Try to treat others and yourself with compassion. The following statements are helpful:

I totally accept and love myself.

I forgive him/her for not being perfect.

I forgive myself for not being perfect.

Now decide what action/answer would serve the best. To decide doing nothing and just breathing is also a possible action.

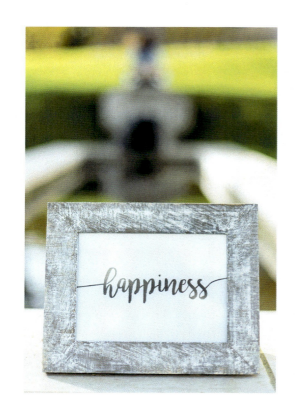

My Second Miracle

Ludwig—my little king

From your birth until now, your presence is huge ever since

Your attention toward connecting with me

I love it so much—it makes me feel free

To express my feelings of being fulfilled

Cuddling, kissing, touching your silky skin

How can a human being be so strong in knowing what he wants?

At the same time so warm, heartfelt, and such a sweet one

Sometimes I experience my limits with you

But at the same time, I admire your personality and how you are living your own truth

In a self-confident way that amazes me every time

Your soul is so strong—you are just right

I feel so connected to your inner being

Helping me accept my own unwanted feelings

Ludwig, you are amazing, and I will always love you!

I grow with and through you every day

Even when I am sometimes feeling anger about your behavior, I think, please, just stay

Please stay as strong and special as you are

Always following your inner self and your heart

Our Children Are Little Buddhas

Little Buddhas everywhere
Smiling, running, and don't care
Living in the moment with their wholeness
Feeling all feelings and do never less
Mindful and shining every day
So cute and adorable – please let this age stay
We should step back and learn from them
Their games and stories are delightful and
When they see something that they like
Everything around them just fades
Always a new adventure
They don't need much to feel frisky and simply
enjoy nature
They are amused by little things

Adults don't even see the butterflies' beautiful wings
With your child, you can discover a new world and
happiness everywhere
Suddenly, you stop thinking about your
problems –
Instead, I don't care
You just experience this moment with your loved
ones
Little Buddha - everywhere runs

Compassion

Lorelei is feeling bad about herself because she thinks she isn't good enough as a mom and should be more compassionate with her children.

Mindful Mom: What is wrong with you?

Lorelei: I am so exhausted. I feel so tired, overwhelmed, and on top of that, even guilty that I cannot be the best mom for my little ones.

Mindful Mom: You need to replenish and recharge so you can be the best version of yourself again. Moms are doing so well in being compassionate with their children and all other loved ones: husband, parents, friends, neighbors, and so on. But first and foremost, we ought to learn to be compassionate with ourselves. Otherwise, we run after the illusion of always being loving and caring and giving without burning out. You are the biggest gift and help for your loved ones and their whole world. You know all their needs and take care of them.

Do you know it for yourself?

Living compassion toward ourselves is a key for being fulfilled, energized, thriving, and uplifting. Then you can be the best mom, spouse, daughter, worker, friend, etc.

Lorelei: So how do I get there?

Mindful Mom: First step, notice all the big and small negative comments, criticism, and bad talk against yourself and the world/conditions around you. Just observe a few days or even longer what is going on in your head, especially in those moments when we feel stressed out, weak, unloved, small, or guilty. Notice what thoughts your mind produces. Try just to notice without being judgmental.

Which leads to the second step: The nonjudgmental noticing is a powerful tool from the practice of mindfulness. You might notice that already that helps you. Because you step back, it creates distance and space between you and your thoughts.

Thoughts are just a part of us.

Most people believe every thought they think and take it as the whole truth. But every thought is created from your past experiences with the intention to protect you because our brain's number one target is to survive. So everything is seen as a potential threat. Therefore, it tends to cling to the negative experiences and create negative scenarios simply to protect us.

But you can rewire your brain toward the positive aspects, paying attention to what is going well, the positive aspects of the day as we practice the gratitude/appreciations exercise. With time, you will notice that you start to feel better because you feed your brain with positive thoughts or affirmations. This is already a part of self-care, which leads me to the big-sector self-care.

Everything you can imagine that is fun for you and replenishes you, do it first thing in the morning. Start with a few minutes and broaden this more and more. This is the ultimate kick-starter in your day. It sets your intention for a good morning and a good day.

Lorelei: I don't know even where to start to take care of myself. And I have many chores. I think I just don't have enough time.

Mindful Mom: This is a restricting belief most people have and keep thinking every day: *I don't have enough time*. The truth is you don't have enough time not to do it. If you continue to sacrifice yourself long term, your stressed body and mind can develop a stress-related disease, you will age faster, and the worst is you just feel awful, unhappy, tired, and exhausted all the time.

Just try it out: For instance, wake up at least five minutes earlier than your children and write down your *I Ams* to set up a positive intention for the day: I am a good mom, I am gratitude, I am joy, etc., whatever makes you feel light, happy, and joyous. Feel then the difference in your body and mind. The raising of your mood and the quality of your day. Then you try to find little gaps throughout the day for taking time for yourself and "recharge."

Lorelei: Okay, five minutes, I can do that. Thank you!

Mindful Mom: You are so welcome and never forget you are a good mom.

How you travel is important
as where you arrive.

—Steven R. Corvey

Being Fulfilled

Waking up with the first thought: Thank you

You can't believe your life is true

The next moment you look at your child's face

Every day just living free and there is no race

Your first agenda is enjoying your lifetime with your kids

All the duties, like laundry, cleaning, cooking, whenever it fits

Taking care of yourself whatever that means

Exercise, meditate, or creating the home of your dreams

Recharge your energy and relish the little things

Following your heart's bells

This is the biggest gift you can give your family

Making yourself happy, number one priority

You can be the best mom and wife

And accomplish whatever you want in your life

Self-Care

Mindful Mom is making herself ready for her Zumba class, putting on her exercise clothes and packing her bag.

Henri and Ludwig: Mom, we do not want you to go.

Mindful Mom: I will be back soon.

Ludwig: No, I don't want you to go. Stay here, please.

Ludwig starts to cry.

Mindful Mom: It's okay, my little treasure, I will be back soon. You know, exercise for Mom is like playing for you. It brings fun, and Mom stays healthy and full of energy so I can play with you so much better. You won't even notice when I am gone. And when I am back, we can play together.

Ludwig calms down, and Mindful Mom can go to the gym.

After the class, she is joyous, enerized and full of happiness.

Mindful Mom: Hey, my best ones, how are you? What would you like to play? I will quickly take a shower. Meanwhile you choose and prepare everything.

The boys are so happy and looking forward to play with their Mom.

You are enough and worthy.
You are a good mom.

Peace

All the good feelings flowing in a loop

Noticing just the blessings around you

When it comes to happiness

I realize more, that it depends on the outside factors less

Doing some exercise in the morning's first bliss

Everything outside is so peaceful and fresh

Just a glimpse above into the sky

Being mindful, no thoughts clinging like "why"

The whole day is set up to be good

The good inner feeling you created is the root

It doesn't matter what problems your mind creates

Your inner being always feels whole, worthy, and freedom that relates

Nothing serious is going on here

You are perfect the way you are

Insert image 22 below this poem

Let Yourself Free

All the thoughts inside me

Guilt, reproaches, worries, and just not being free

Insecurities not having enough skills for your own breakthrough

Letting you feel like you don't have a clue

But being aware that thoughts create your feelings

You can switch every time as you need it

I choose to be happy, no matter what

I choose to feel confident and trust

I choose not to doubt and feel free

To do anything I need to be the real me

Could be your new mantras whenever a stressful thought arises

Instead of beating yourself up, praise!

Praise everything and everyone that crosses your path

You will notice there is a huge power in that

Your thoughts are just a part of you

You are so much more in this beautiful truth

In every moment, you can choose how you would like to feel

Tell yourself good feeling things, and soon it becomes real

Negative feelings are wasted energy

Stop doing it daily and let yourself free

You are enough and worthy.
You are a good mom.

The Wouldn't It Be Nice Game

Henri asks Mindful Mom: Should we play our funny game "Wouldn't it be nice"?

Mindful Mom: Yes, sure, that would be awesome! You start, go ahead!

Henri: Wouldn't it be nice if it snows tomorrow?

Mindful Mom: Wouldn't it be nice if we could go on a trip soon and everything goes well?

Henri: Wouldn't it be nice if I would have a great idea for Ludwig's birthday?

Mindful Mom: Wouldn't it be nice if we could get some new plants for our garden?

[...]

Next morning, Henri runs to wake up Mindful Mom and is beaming all over his face. "Mom, Mom, it is snowing!"

A few months later, the family came back from a nine-day road trip through America, and they feel blessed; everything went well and smoothly, and they will never forget the incredible experiences.

[...]

What will your name be— a strong and royal name it should be

What decision we are going to make—your dad and me

Which gives you freedom, love, and trust in yourself

Something special, full of life's abundance and wealth

I know we will find the perfect name for you

When we experience your personality, it will be true

Your brothers love you already

Giving you kisses and giving my belly pats every day

Ludwig talks about sharing with you his bed

It's gorgeous to see him sharing without becoming mad

Oh, I have the pictures already in my mind

Feeding you and holding you, loving and kind

That's why life is so worthy

I can't imagine it without you already

Another miracle is heading to us

A new soul, a new person without any rush

I notice it has started to snow

Dreaming about you with a feeling of a blissful flow

You are enough and worthy.
You are a good mom.

51

Living Gratitude

Henri, in the evening before going to bed: Shall we say what we are grateful for?

Ludwig: I want too!

Mindful Mom: Yes, sure. Everyone says one thing, and then we are going around.

Henri: I am grateful that Daddy is always playing with us Playmobil.

Ludwig: I am grateful that we have a trumpet.

Mindful Mom: I am grateful that we were outside today and had fun in the snow.

Henri: I am grateful that I can always go to tae kwon do.

Ludwig: I am grateful for our trumpet.

Henri: You say always the same. We don't even have a trumpet.

Ludwig: Yes, we do. Daddy is the trumpet.

Everybody laughs out loud.

Mindful Mom: I am grateful that we had such fresh and delicious lunch today.

Henri: I am grateful that we have such an awesome life here in America.

Ludwig: I am grateful that we have a drum.

Henri: Who is the drum?

Ludwig: Grandpa.

Everyone laughs.

Mindful Mom: I am grateful that I am blessed to be your mom.

Henri: I am grateful that our neighbor cat Socks visited us today.

[ ]

Everyone goes happy to bed and feels so blessed because you are aware of so many things that you can be thankful for. Another mindful evening full of gratitude and appreciation.

There are no mistakes, only opportunities.

—Tina Fey

I am Heartfulness

What is your life's purpose?

What are your values flowing through and are so close?

So close to your heart and everything that's important to you

Connect as often as you can with your inner truth

Take time and ask yourself about your vision

Go through every area of life and listen

By doing so, I feel good feelings overflow me

Almost as if I am all the time free

To follow my path, no matter what

To trust and never giving up

I am heartfulness as a mantra in my head

I feel how my whole body resonates with that

I feel motivated to expand myself and my passion

Mindfulness and self-growth are my obsession

I feel so comfortable by being me

Never ever it felt so easy just to be

Just find a word that resonates with you the most

You will be your happiness-life host

Ready to receive all the gifts

That life gives you because of your own bliss

The snow is flying so peacefully, the stillness inside the house

My best ones are taking their nap, I savor the quietness around

But also, I do have to smile when I think about when they awake

Always ready for joy, focus, and play

Always smiling and living in the present moment and state

How wonderful is this feeling of faith

How your brilliant brain works

Another morning when Mindful Mom awakes at 6:00 a.m. She could stay longer in her bed; it is so warm and cozy. But she decides to get up. Five, four, three, two, one, and she stands up. What is her driving force? She tells her mind she wants it. She is telling her mind what to do instead of doing what the mind tells her, like *you can do it later, it is too early to stand up, everyone is sleeping, just stay and enjoy a half hour more.* But Mindful Mom knows she is the best version of herself when she takes care of herself and feeding this other fire inside her besides loving to be a mom. She wants to teach. She wants to share with the world her passion, inspire people, give her knowledge further, to help other moms grow and to enjoy their parenting—the most beautiful gift of having children.

So she tells her mind, *I want to write that book. I love writing it. I enjoy writing it. This is an amazing book. This is an extraordinary book. I love it. I want it, I want it. I can sleep later. I am fit and inspired to get it done. And I have chosen to write that book.*

She empowers herself by using *choose* instead of *need* or *must*.

She remembers the rules of the mind:

First: the mind does what it thinks you want it to do. You need to communicate with your mind properly and more positive than you do usually. By saying to your mind you are too tired, you will do it later, you are too exhausted, it will follow and let your body feel exactly like that. But you can choose the opposite: Tell your mind better things, and it will follow either directive. We have a brilliant mind that you can rewire and reinstall all the things that you need to grow, would like to succeed and accomplish.

Second: Your mind does what is familiar. So make things that are unfamiliar familiar. You would like to take care of yourself and do yoga/exercise/jog/eat better/be more creative? Do it, and do it the first thing in the morning. After a while, it starts to become familiar, and you have created a new habit that your mind and body do not want to miss anymore. And when you cheer yourself up with supporting thoughts like *I have chosen it, I love it, I want it, I am doing great*, the mind changes.

When you change the thought, you change your feeling, and then you are acting in a different way.

First, you change your habits, and then your personality changes. You become that person you have always wanted to be. So tell your mind whatever you would like to change and go for it!

And don't forget to praise yourself. Always praise yourself, cheer up, sing songs about how great you are as you are doing it with your children.

Let-Your-Mind-Work-for-You Tool: Watch your thoughts and the language you use all day long. Tell your mind better things about yourself, others, and everything you would like to accomplish. Choose words that make you excited. After a while, you will notice how the patterns in your brain rewire (neuroplasticity) and positive changes start to emerge. Research shows that unfamiliar things turn to a new habit after around sixty-six days. Hang in there for at least three weeks and see the results.

You are enough and worthy.
You are a good mom.

Little Mindful Miracles

Ohh, those children, how beautiful they are

Beaming almost all the time in their own world

No matter what happens, they switch back to their bliss and feel alive

Never worrying—it does not change things anyway

Being present in the moment—everything is okay

In the littlest thing, they find a whole world to explore

While adults think they need so much more

Always on top of their game

Not having time for our children's bliss—it's a shame

Say out loud "I love you"

As often as you can because it's true

The unconditional love to our children is almighty

Could we feel it for ourselves—we would be free

There is so much our kids can remind us of

Being mindful, not judgmental, and free from rush

Just being instead of doing with all your senses

Seeing the world through children's lenses

So innocent and joyous all day long

In their world nothing seems to be wrong

Anna Meiwes

BE SILLY. BE HONEST. BE KIND.

- *Ralph Waldo Emerson*

Raise your energy

Mindful Mom created a list of things that recharge her, make her feel good, lighthearted, inspired, and in a state of flow:

- Being creative (writing, poetry, creating/ preparing presents for others)
- Decorating inside and outside the house
- Listening to favorite music (she has a list that she continues to fill up)
- Dancing (Zumba or to her favorite music)
- Clowning around with her kids
- Playing with her kids, hockey, soccer, games
- Painting with her kids
- Writing postcards to loved ones
- Surprising others
- Helping others (neighbors, friends, loved ones, foreigners)
- Being generous (giving things that she doesn't need or have too much away/ donating)

- Personal growth - learning something new (an instrument, new insights about her passion topics/online classes, etc.)
- Creating her soul-business
- Teaching other people and inspiring them
- Relaxation (autogenic training/ progressive muscle relaxation/yoga)
- Meditation (guided and by herself)
- Reading inspiring books/magazines
- Listening to inspiring podcasts/ interviews
- Painting furniture
- Being mindful (experiences/doing ordinary things like cooking or cleaning/ practicing mindfulness with thoughts, feelings/being mindful in the present moment with herself and others)
- Talking to loved ones and spending time with them
- Exercise
- Jogging

- Being outside in nature
- Enjoying every weather, especially snow/going barefoot through the snow/grass
- Always smiling and beaming
- Fresh cooking
- Watching photobooks
- Practicing gratitude and appreciation through journaling every day
- Letting go of a bad feeling thought: *Is that really truth? What's the evidence? Does that thought serve me right now? It is just a thought.*
- Breathing (every hour and before reading a text message or answering: a deep breath in and out/5-3-5 while waiting for the computer loadings/a call/someone to come/in a line/in a road construction/at the doctor's office/other offices, etc.)
- Decluttering and sorting things out – donating
- Organizing and hosting a community event like *"SoulSisters"*
- Meeting like-minded people/family and friends
- Traveling
- Crafting
- Trying out new things (going new ways, new restaurants, new skill, new sport, etc.)
- Singing (by herself, with her children, in a choir)
- Thinking good thoughts and not believing depressing thoughts
- Living kindness (giving money to people who need it; preparing gifts, unexpected surprises; giving compliments as much as possible to everyone who crosses her way; uplifting others)
- **DOING WHAT SHE IS PASSIONATE ABOUT EVERY DAY**

She thinks about other things that other moms might like to do to raise their energy, like sewing, knitting, gardening, making jewelry, supporting people in a hospice/assisted living/children's homes, etc.

What kind of things do YOU enjoy?
What makes YOU happy, lighthearted, and feel fulfilled?
CREATE YOUR OWN LIST!

Thoughts

Why do we believe our bad-feeling thoughts?

We tend to think everything is true—all the odds

Our brain produces thoughts based on every experience we had

To protect us, stories that made us mad

Mad at yourself or others, and we blame both

Feeling unworthy and not enough

Pondering, worrying, and feeling frustrated

Can lead to feeling depressed and very self-related

So tell your mind better stories and "lies"

You will notice the difference with time

Notice when you feel negative and stuck

Before that feeling came an untrue thought that you can unwrap

Awareness is the first step that would be enough

Then you can choose to think less about not serving stuff

Asking your brain questions like: Does that thought serve me right now?

What actions would serve me and how?

What perception can I use to see it in a different way?

The negative one stops sticking like clay

You discover a less negative one that helps you out of your story

Always seeing the best instead of your worry

No matter what situation stresses you out

Watch your thoughts and you can get out of your dark cloud

Toward a silver lining that feels so good and lighthearted

You give up your resistance toward not being perfect

Every time your children make you upset

Watch your thought and become aware of that

Your thoughts about the event create your feelings

Acknowledge them and stop them feeding

Through awareness the feeling can flow

As next step, find a serving one for you to grow

After a while, it becomes second nature

You free yourself—this is a game-changer

Be happy in the moment.
That's enough. Each moment is all we need, not more.

— *Mother Teresa*

BREATHE

Your Children's negative emotions

Lorelei: I don't know how to deal with the worries and anxiety of my older one. He is sometimes so overwhelmed. When he is worried, I am worried. I don't know how to react, except by trying to comfort him.

Mindful Mom: It's important to support your child by staying with the feeling of negative emotions like anger, frustration, resentment, and fear. Parents tend to get rid of those feelings as quickly as possible because they don't feel comfortable with them either. They were also taught by their parents unconsciously, that negative emotions are not okay, for example by sending them to their room when they would have a tantrum. So, every time they see or experience negative emotions and try to shut them down, the children get the message that those emotions aren't "good" or are even "bad." Therefore, as adults, we try to escape from these "negative/bad/not wanted" feelings as soon as possible through distractions, like food, TV, social media, etc. But that just empowers the feeling for the next time. If you would go on that way for a long time, it can even lead to anxiety or depression.

Lorelei: Then how can I teach my child to deal with it better?

Mindful Mom: First, you take care of yourself. That means every time you experience an unwanted feeling, you practice staying with it. Feel it, acknowledge it, you can even speak with it.

For example, is there a message in that or what does the feeling want to protect you from or teach you?

And then you let it go. You can use breathing or other mindful techniques to release it. Feelings have a purpose. They *want* to be felt, embraced, welcomed, and then released. Sometimes we get more clarity or more power through experiencing a strong feeling.

With your child, you can practice dealing with difficult feelings by explaining that the fear/anxiety is like a big brother or sister who tries to protect you and to take care of you. You can practice talking to that feeling, like, *Hello, fear, I know you are trying to protect me. It is okay you are there. But I know I am safe, and I can handle the situation. You may go now.*

Every time your child feels restless, fearless, or anxious you can repeat that kind of talk.

With anger, it helps singing about it and/or dancing. It helps release being caught up in the heaviness of that feeling.

Every time I do it with the boys, at some point, they start laughing and the situation switches from anger and frustration to lightheartedness.

Savoring

When Mindful Mom has with her kids dessert, they would do a mindfulness exercise.

Mindful Mom: Come on, my best ones, we will do our savoring exercise. So take a bite and then close your eyes. Now tell me what do you taste. Is it sweet, bitter, salty, or sour? What can you say about the surface? Is it hard or soft? What kinds of forms do you taste? Is it actually tasty for you?

Ludwig: Hmm, it tastes awesome! It is sweet and hard and soft at the same time. It is chocolate!

Mindful Mom: Yes, Ludwig, but it isn't so important to really name it. Just the awareness to one sense helps us being mindful and really enjoy our food. Really taste all the nuances and flavors. Being aware how thankful we may be for this delicious dessert.

Henri: It tastes like milk, cocoa, sweet, and like nuts.

Mindful Mom: Yes, now try to move around the next piece with your tongue and try to sense the different forms, surface, quality, and how it changes with time.

Ludwig: It's melting, I like it!

The boys like doing this so much, almost every meal they start to do the exercises on their own und a have a lot of fun.

Savoring Tool: You can choose whatever you like: a raisin, a piece of fruit, your daily food, even a nip of water will do. Close your eyes and be aware of the taste, the form, the flavors, the ingredients, maybe even memories may arise. Notice everything you can without judging or pondering.

Taking time for mindful eating and savoring enhances gratitude, enjoyment, and intuitive eating. A nice by-product is you start eating less and healthier. Furthermore, it counteracts our brain's hedonic adaptation (our brain gets used to every experience after a short time).

Friendship

All together—moments forever

Small and big things sharing with each other

Endless bliss flowing through you

And you think this can't be true

Friends so close, how wonderful

Similar values, tastes, and family rules

Our little ones are playing and singing

Having fun, insights, and learning sharing

We enjoy them—our greatest treasures—so much

Running, clowning around, reading, and having ice cream with fudge

I feel so grateful for these souls in our lives

It's so worthy those moments with people that we incredibly like

Book of Appreciations

Before sleeping, Mindful Mom would think and write down, savoring all the things she is grateful for that day:

playing soccer with my boys and laughing out loud while playing, the great sunny weather and being outside for almost two hours, enjoying the neighbor's cat sitting on my lap and petting him, nice and lovely conversations with the neighbors, another neighbor called to ask how we are, cooking fresh three times and preparing a nice and healthy meal for my family, enjoying a delicious green shake, having had two hours for myself before the kids got up, doing yoga, working on my business, writing poems, a walk alone in the morning darkness and enjoying the fresh air, thinking good and uplifting thoughts, the little ones' laughter on the swing, being fit and full of energy almost all day long, sorting out paper stuff, that felt awesome, kissing and cuddling with my husband after he arrived home—our new ritual to connect and strengthen our relationship, being such a good team as parents, taking a long shower and enjoying the scent of the shower gel, enjoying a delicious ice cream, doing relaxations, meditating to prepare for birth, attending an online seminar and getting new insights that motived me, collecting information about publishing a book, cuddling and kissing my children, being really mindful during bedtime routines and saying "good night."

While writing down those things she is grateful for, she takes time to really go back to those moments she is appreciating with all the little details.

She imagines the awareness from that moment and savors the experience again. While savoring, she is feeling so thankful, so blessed and fulfilled, that she falls asleep with a feeling of awesomeness and a peaceful smile on her face. And her last thought is *How blessed I am—THANK YOU.*

You are enough and worthy.
You are a good mom.

Be happy in the moment.
That's enough. Each moment is all we need, no more.

—Mother Teresa

Everything Is Always Working Out For Us

No matter what life gives you

You make the decision if it is really true

How do you react to this event?

Is your mind telling you could it prevent?

Or do you choose to make the best of it?

Giving the event less power, not trying to evade

Instead, tell yourself, "Everything is always working out for us"

"I can do it, no reason to rush"

Lifting yourself to more confidence

Is melting away your resistance

Resistance to circumstances you cannot change

Acceptance and mindfulness give you strength

Choose mantras, thoughts that delight you and give you a smile

Do it, claim it, code it in for a while

You will notice the things you do

Change your feelings toward the things that happen and give you more flow

It's a matter of practice being aware of your thoughts

Toward yourself, others, and your words

Think different, think things that delight and feel good

Instead of anything you think you shouldn't have done or you should

Everything is working out for you

Repeat it over and over, and it will become true

Learn to enjoy every minute of
your life. Be happy now.

——*Earl Nightingale*

Self-love

Henri: Mom, what does it mean to self-love?

Mindful Mom: When you love yourself, everything becomes easier. You don't blame yourself or others. You appreciate yourself and others and everything you have.

We practice that with our great *gratitude ritual* in the evening, for example, and being mindful with our food when we are savoring it.

Henri: I love our *"enjoying the dessert"* time!

Mindful Mom: Sometimes it means to stop yourself from doing what you want and instead doing what you need, like when your *brain or body says*, "Oh, I want more and more chocolate, I do not want to stop," but you know you need to stop eating it because overeating and too much sugar isn't good for your body.

You remember how the body-police is always pleased when we eat healthy food like vegetables and nuts and are drinking enough water? Then the body-police become extraordinarily strong to protect us. We stay healthy, fit, and full of energy.

Henri: Yes, they turn into a SWAT team when we eat healthy and spend a lot of time outside!

Mindful Mom: Exactly. It is a part of self-care. Furthermore, self-care is doing daily what is healthy for you, like exercise, proper sleep, having friendships, helping others, and—

Henri: I know, I know! And having fun!

Mindful Mom: Indeed! Therefore, Mom is going to Zumba, meeting her friends, going to the gym, jogging, writing, and working as a life coach. That is fun, and I stay healthy and strong for being able to play with you.

Sometimes self-love means also to say "no" when you feel in your inner gut that something isn't the right thing for you to do. Imagine a good friend of yours, for example Archer, is asking you to make fun of another classmate. You don't want to disappoint Archer, but at the same time, you feel around your belly an unpleasant feeling because you know that would be mean. That's a situation to say "no." Even if Archer becomes angry at you, you practiced self-love because you protected your own values, no matter what others expect from you.

Henri: How do I know which friends are the right ones?

Mindful Mom: Just be aware of how you feel when you are together. Do you have fun together? Do you feel uplifted and at ease? Or do they make you feel bad, small, and shy, laughing at you? It's okay when friends are sometimes challenging so you can grow, but most of the time you should feel comfortable and supported and having a good time with them.

Henri: Okay, I think I like all my friends.

Mindful Mom: There are two more things about self-love.

You remember when we do our *forgotten-and-forgiven sign* when we are arguing or something happened that annoyed us?

Henri: Yes, I like our *peace sign*, and Ludwig is so sweet when he is doing it.

Mindful Mom: Self-love means to forgive yourself and others. Every human being makes mistakes. Sometimes we are very angry at others, for example, when Ludwig took your toy away or you hit each other. That's absolutely not okay, but after every situation like that, where you feel it wasn't right, you may forgive immediately, learn from it, and grow through that experience.

And the last thing I would like to point out when it comes to self-love is living with purpose.

You remember when I always say every human being needs to find out what is their passion and their unique talents that make it fun to serve people with these unique talents and passion?

Henri: Yes, you say Daddy is managing and improving everything in his company so the company can produce great things for others.

Mindful Mom: Exactly. He was still studying after finishing school and discovered his passion and his talents, so he worked a lot to get there, to be successful on his own terms, and is still learning. And me, I discovered holistic health, stress management, relaxation, and self-growth first for myself as I expected you. So I learned from my studies more and more to be the best mom for you! And now I teach other people how to deal with stress, grow in health and happiness. It's my passion and is so much fun!

You must choose and set goals for how you would like to live in your life, then you can be proud of yourself and feel great about yourself, feeling good enough and worthy. Then you can accomplish anything you want!

When we think about what you are proud of yourself after our appreciation ritual, we practice that!

Henri: Mom, I love you so much!

Mindful Mom: I love you too, my treasure! Always remember you need to love yourself! Always, no matter what.

Strengthen-Your-Self-Love Tools:

Every time you acted in a way you did not want to, breathe in and out slowly, say "I forgive myself," let it go, and restart.

Write down at the end of the day every little and big thing you did/accomplished and say "thank you" to yourself.

Praise yourself after every task you do, and in front of a mirror, say uplifting and nice things to yourself. Say things that you would like to hear from others to yourself—it works wonder.

Self-Doubts

Every mom has those moments

Feeling guilty of not being perfect

Not being patient enough

Feeling this heaviness on her chest

Have been too strict on her loved ones

Lost her temper because of a minor cause

Expressed anger and frustration toward her kids

It feels so painful inside her guts

She is beating herself up for having done these mistakes

How can I treat the best in my life that way for God's sake?

She regrets yelling and exploding in front of them

Thinking she is a horrible mom

Feeling awful in the midst of anger, resentment, and emotional chaos

Frustrated at herself and so lost

But after a while, a silver lining comes into her mind

Moms are also human beings—they might

They might make mistakes

Adoptive thoughts come like I am still okay

I am doing my best in the very moment

A feeling of relief without any comment

Tears run upon her face

She thinks, my mistakes and weaknesses, I may embrace

A feeling of being accepted and loved unconditionally

Like I treat my family

I will try to treat me

Be my own mom and parenting myself

Suddenly, she starts to feel free and inner wealth

Allow herself to have both sides

The ones she likes and the ones she dislikes

Isn't that the whole truth?

Acceptance toward yourself and you start go

Going to be the best version of yourself

Through forgiveness and coming back to the present moment

Mindfully being aware of the present experience

Not judging but appreciating everything

Super Daddy

You are their playmate and protector

Their supporter and care giver

Loving and caring like a mom

At the same time so strong behind them

Playing with the children so much

Since they were born and from the first touch

No fear dealing with anything

I remember as you took our first born confident like a king

You are born to be a dad

Always joyous and never sad

Doing everything that is needed for their happiness

I know they will remember you later as the best

Because you are spending so much time with them

Honest, being full there, mindfully playing, having fun

Nothing comes in between your strong connection's way

You nurture your own little child when you play

I see and love this sparkle in your and our children's eyes and hearts

It's fulfilling to be this family's part

The best parenting, I can imagine with you

You are Super Daddy—this is absolutely true

You are enough and worthy.
You are a good dad.

77

MY HUSBAND

I love how wise you are. Often, when I learn something new about happiness, I realize that you are that way naturally. I respect and admire you.

I love being your wife, and I feel honored to be your soulmate, your significant other. I love it when you surprise me with a new magazine or book about happiness, mindfulness, or self-growth. I love seeing you with our children, how you do funny and crazy things with them, how you play Playmobil together, totally lost in the game, laughing, screaming, and enjoying time together. I love the fact that you are *my husband and that we have three wonderful boys.*

I like it so much when you prepare food for me—you did it from the first day we met. I remember how lovely you prepared bread roles when I was an intern. I love our conversations about the world and what is really important. I like listening to you when you explain Lean Management and things like *Toyota Kata* to me, I am almost an expert, just kidding! I like it how you compare difficult stuff with soccer examples so everyone can relate and understand it better. I like it when you do your notes on little sheets of paper of used envelopes or old papers. I love how you look in your sleeping underwear, especially the one you wear since we met and the one, I gave you at your last birthday. I appreciate all the things you do for me, for our three awesome boys, and everyone else around you. When we have family or friends over, you always take care of them. You are such a great host. The best thing about it is that you then also take care of our kids so I can totally relax and enjoy conversations and interactions with our visitors—I love that, and I am so grateful about that fact.

I love your smile that enlightens the whole room and is over your whole face. I love kissing your face and your nose. I love how we *fight* with each other in a playful way until we laugh. Of course, I am in love with the way you look. You are tall and handsome. I remember when my family met you the first time. They were amazed how handsome you are. You would remind them of Prince William. I am totally in love with you and had never thought that it is possible to fell in love a few times with the same person. I did it with you on our way back from Paris in your first car, on our road trip in Arizona as we had breakfast at the Lake Havasu, and in Detroit as we enjoyed time on the river. I believe enjoying life together and with our children, following our hearts, being mindful for each other, and having fun are the reasons we are so happy.

I am so grateful that I may share my life with you. Thank you.

What do you love about your husband/partner/significant other?

Write it down and feel all the good feelings that come up.

79

Rejection

Everyone fears rejection

All fears come from it and your reactions

Who can reject you? Ask yourself for real

A critical person that is mean?

Anger, frustration, the tenseness in your body

Your mind and thought circuits are telling you just a story

But the only person that has power over you

Is reading this right now though!

If you don't let it in

Nobody and nothing can you ruin

Decide to not accept the negative comments of others

Step back, it is just an opinion that doesn't really matter

The only thing that matters is the things you tell yourself

Uplifting, positive, and strong words bring you inner wealth

You are here for a reason

Henri: Mom, I do not want Daddy to go to work. It is always so great if he is at home and spends time with us, plays with us.

Mindful Mom: I know, Henri, it is the best when we are all together and enjoying time together. I love having Daddy at home too, but every human being has a purpose in his life. You are given special qualities, your unique talent. With that ability, you can serve others in a way that just you can do. When you find out what you love to do and what you are good at, that is your unique talent.

See, Daddy is incredibly good in improving things in companies, and he treats every person with respect and kindness. This mixture is his unique talent. And he has fun at work like you when you are playing. He experiences happiness when he achieves something at his work and can serve his company and the people that work there. Therefore, he is extraordinarily successful by doing what he loves, what he is passionate about, and serving others.

Henri: What can I do later?

Mindful Mom: You can do whatever you decide feels right for you. What do you think you are good at and is fun for you?

Henri: I am good at playing Playmobil and being a big brother.

Mindful Mom: Yes, absolutely, you are a good leader and truly kind and loving when it comes to playing with your little brother. Who knows, maybe you can later develop new Playmobil toys and create Playmobil worlds and serve other children with that so they can have fun as much as you when you play.

Henri, beaming: Yeah, that sounds good!

In the evening, before going to bed, after the gratitude ritual, Mindful Mom deepens Henri's interest in talking about his purpose.

Mindful Mom: Henri, my treasure, I would like to try out something new with you. Are you up to that?

Henri: Yes, yes. What is it, Mom?

Mindful Mom: You remember we talked about Daddy's work today, do you? I would like to ask you a few questions about you.

How did you make a good difference today? What do you think, through what acts, for example?

Henri: Hmm, I helped Ludwig with putting his clothes on and brushing his teeth.

Mindful Mom: Exactly, you were truly kind and helpful. Also, do you remember what you did when Daddy and I had an argument?

Henri: No, what did I do? What do you mean?

Mindful Mom: You came to us and noticed the tensed atmosphere between us and asked what is wrong. Afterward, you tried to calm us down and said funny things to us, so we had to smile. That made such a difference, and we made up.

Henri: Oh yes, that was funny!

Mindful Mom: What talent did you uncover in this situation would you say?

Henri: I can reconcile?

Mindful Mom: Absolutely. Additionally, you are incredibly good at sensing people when something is wrong between them. Your talents here are being sensitive and uplifting others.

What did you do to make someone else feel special today?

Henri: I know, I know. I was cheering and clapping when Ludwig got his tenth sticker. He was laughing and happy that I was singing, clapping, and happy for him.

Mindful Mom: Exactly. He was so proud of himself, and you helped him through your kind behavior and truly being happy for him to feel special. Your talent here was again to uplift others.

Was there anything—a lesson, a gift, a nice experience—that made *you* feel special today?

Henri: Yes, as I was at the violin lesson and I could remember everything and was holding the violin right. It was so much fun to play violin.

Mindful Mom: That sounds wonderful, Henri. You see, that could mean that being creative with music and learning new things is something that is important to you and it is fun for you.

If you like, we can talk about those things from time to time or every day from now on?

Henri: Yes, please, Mom, I would like that.

Mindful Mom: Okay, my little treasure, now I will sing our song for you:

I will love you forever

I will like you for always

As long as I am living, my baby you will be.

(*Love you forever* by Robert Munsch)

Good night, I love you so much. I am so happy to be your mom and that I am privileged to be your mom. You are so lovable and such a great boy! I love you. Good night.

Henri: Good night, Mom! I love you too.

Every Word In My Head

Notice the talk inside your mind

Is it negative, destructive, or kind?

All words you think or say

Are an affirmation and as if you would pray

Our thoughts determine our feelings

It depends on your attaching of meaning

You can always decide how to review the situation

No matter what, anger or frustration

Every experience is worthy somehow

When you recognize this truth, it sets you free now

Be aware how you talk to yourself

Notice about everyone and everything your inner comments

Mindful Mom –
Two insights

It is Monday morning, and you wake up with your first thoughts, worries, duties that come into your mind: laundry, vacuum, groceries, appointments, calls, work, household, etc. I should have done this. I could have done that better. I don't look good. Oh my gosh! My hair, my skin, I could lose weight, and so on. What can I cook today? Something healthy, fresh, and simple to prepare. Oh man, every day this dilemma with cooking. Oh, today my friend has a birthday. I can't forget it and do need to get a present. Oh man, I hope I can manage everything today. And the circle of all kinds of things begins to turn. Just five minutes you are awake, and you already feel stressed out, under pressure, and rushing. Thinking about all that stuff, all you must do while making the bed, brushing teeth, and waking up the kids, not even noticing your child's smiling face because he is happy to see you.

Rushing from room to room, doing everything as fast as possible, "to save time" *your mind says to you*. And suddenly, your cell phone falls down and breaks! What the! you think. And at the same time, your kids have an argument, are yelling at each other, and you just feel this anger in your gut, not knowing how to manage it all. After screaming, yelling, crying, punishing your kids and feeling guilty about it, you are sitting at breakfast, and a thought flows into your mind: appointment, dentist, kids, today, in fifteen minutes, oh no!

Come on, kids, we need to hurry up. You put at least something edible in your mouth and swallow it almost in one piece while motivating the kids to brush their teeth. Somehow you are standing in the bathroom and the kids are brushing. Wow! What a glimpse of a relaxed five minutes and well-behaved children. But the next challenge is coming. They are having so much fun with water and just don't want to stop running it. You are getting tensed and more tensed, every minute more they don't listen to you, until you find yourself yelling at them and afterward again feeling guilty about it. *I am a bad mom*, your critical mind says. The day goes on, and you feel yourself being in a hamster wheel rushing to and from appointments, work, picking up kids, errands, and duties.

In the evening, you feel so exhausted that you think the only thing you can do is sit on the couch, consuming unhealthy stuff (*your mind tells you, I totally deserve it after such a hard day*) while living your favorite TV show addiction on TV. And before you fall asleep your last thoughts are "What a horrible day," "I feel terrible," "Another day I couldn't make everything on my to-do list," "I could have done this in a much better way," "I yelled at my adorable children," "Oh no, I forgot my friend's birthday, darn it!" Thoughts that make you feel guilty, depressed, unworthy, and not being enough.

The next morning you feel bad, and the same thoughts continue. The same procedure every day—as always.

BREAK.

Oh my gosh, just a dream, luckily, thank God! You wake up and think, *Today it's gonna be an awesome day! This is a good morning. This is a really good morning. Today I will follow my inner voice, enjoy the day with my loved ones, and be the best friend for myself.* You start to think about all the big and little things that you are thankful for: your children, your bed, your home, being blessed, being a mom, your friends, and the singing birds.

Your children and your husband are still sleeping, and you decide to exercise and go jogging. But before you stand up, you do a little morning meditation and take a "self-love bath" in your mind. While you are jogging, you use a mantra that induces some good feelings inside you, like "I love being a mom," "I feel good," "I like being me." After a short time, you arrive, your loved ones are still sleeping, and you decide to drink a coffee and walk barefoot on your backyard's grass. Oh, it feels awesome. You feel connected as if the whole world is open for you and embraces you. You think you can accomplish anything. You feel so good and relaxed and in a state of flow that you feel like you could write a poem or do something else creative.

After your morning routine, you feel so happy and are so looking forward to greeting your loved ones. Your kids run into your arms, you say "good morning" mindfully, and you kiss and hug them. Your husband is very pleased that you already prepared his coffee and his breakfast and is smiling at you as the best woman in the world. With gratitude and being aware of his blessing, he too can start his day in a mood full of joy.

While you are eating breakfast, your children aren't motivated to eat the healthy stuff. But you feel patient and strong to inspire them and invite them by telling a story about the "body's police" who would need all the healthy vitamins in fruits and vegetables to be strong and be capable against all the pathogens that can make us sick. Your children are so fascinated with that story that it becomes your routine to make use of that story, and it is no more a problem to eat healthy food.

You remember today is your friend's birthday, and you prepared a present already two weeks ago, and you also consider the children's dental appointment. As usual, kiddos aren't that motivated to brush their teeth. But you know once again how to motivate them, so you create a teeth-brushing song. You have so much fun together while brushing teeth you almost can't believe it, relaxed and energized you arrive at the dentist. Everything goes well, including the doing of all your errands, visiting your friend, and being aware of his being touched by your thoughtful present, later preparing a nourishing lunch. When the little ones do their napping, you do a short meditation for fifteen minutes and a relaxation exercise so your body can recharge for the second part of the day.

You feel renewed and full of power and decide to call friends to come over with their children. After having them, which was so much fun with so much laughter and strengthening your friendship, connection, you prepare the kids for going to bed.

With the teeth-brushing song, they are delighted and motivated. You read a good-night story, around all your adorable children. And as they cuddle with you and listen so fascinated, you can't believe how blessed you are!

Before falling asleep, you are doing with them the gratitude ritual and speak about everything they are grateful for. This is the best part of your day because you hear from your children what things they appreciate about the day and you as a mom. "I am grateful that you are always so patient, and I am grateful for playing with our friends today, and I am grateful that we are best friends." With such a deep feeling of love, you say "good night" to every child and feel simply happy and at peace.

You feel still energized and ask yourself, What would I like to do—a walk, plan the next vacation with my husband, write a poem, create a photobook from our last year?

And you listen, which impulse feels the most right and fun for you, then you follow it. Before you fall asleep, you feel fulfilled and blessed and happy. You think about the day and feel so grateful. With a big smile and looking forward to the next day, you fall asleep.

Which version do
YOU
want to live?

What Is Your Why?

What is the fuel that gives you a smile?
Ponder about that question for a while
The reason to continue every day
You will find your own and worthy way
To get more insights from your inner self
Discover all the treasures of the parent's wealth
Why would you want to grow as a parent?
Mindful moments stay in your heart forever
Make sure every day to do what you are
passionate about
First, a little bit for yourself and then everybody of
your circle around

Do whatever is necessary to feel good
Inspired, fulfilled, full of joy—and not through food
What gives you energy and uploads your heart
Is it being creative in some way or any art?
If you find that answer for you

You can manage your day with your inner truth
Feeling at peace, content, and blessed
Feeling good, worthy, and rested
Having this wonderful feeling of having and being
enough
Being a good mom, wife, and full of trust

Last thoughts

I hope you enjoyed the journey of Mindful Mom and could see yourself in her. Every mother is a heroine, a goddess, an angel, and the most important person in her children's world.

My heart's desire is to remind you that you are amazing daily! You are enough, worthy, and a good mom! You are always, always doing your best! Stop criticizing yourself, and instead, start praising and uplifting yourself. Treat yourself as your best friend or your own loving and caring mom.

Rather than asking yourself if you did enough, screening your day for failures, thank yourself for all the thousands of big and little things you are doing for your loved ones, family, friends, neighbors, community, or wherever you are a part of. Notice how many beautiful things you do every day. To whom do you listen? How many times are you helping and soothing others, nourishing, hugging, kissing, caring, and loving? You are smart, diligent, intelligent, loving, and kind, just wonderful the way you are.

Use strategies to remind yourself how amazing you are. Take care of yourself every day and never ever beat up on yourself for things you think you did wrong.

Say to yourself things like "already forgiven and forgotten," "I am still a good mom," "I always do my best" and let it go. Don't waste energy on negatives. We can only be the best version of ourselves if we lift ourselves, take care of ourselves physically and emotionally.

Take care of your thoughts, release bad feelings and stress-making thoughts about yourself and others that do not serve you. Find thoughts *that make you feel lighthearted, full of joy, and strengthen you. Repeat them over and over.*

You will see if you start to change from the inside, your outside starts to change likewise: your children will be more relaxed, all your relationships may benefit from it, you may even get a better job.

But most of all, you'll start enjoying your worthy life. You'll start feeling fulfilled and more and more at peace with the world around you and with yourself. You will feel more powerful, energized, and as your true self, compassionate, loving, caring, joyous, and comfortable being yourself. You will start feeling that all you do is feeding your soul, the souls around you, and your life. You'll live to the full extent instead of "existing" or "sleepwalking," instead of reacting and being hypnotized through our habits, thoughts, and actions that don't serve us and make us feel unhappy.

With time, you learn to repattern and rewire your brain, trying and practicing new things that feel good to you. First, you do it, and then it becomes natural and second nature. Rehearse self-care every morning.

Don't let yourself awake in twenty years and wonder if this is the life you wanted to live, if you lived your dreams, if you lived on your own terms of happiness, if you fully enjoyed your children when they were little, if you enjoyed being a mom. Do not wait, take action, do things that feed your soul as often as possible.

Start where you are, start small, and make it with consistency and then grow from there. Your health and well-being will thank you for it.

If I were to take all these points and put them into a single sentence, this would be it:

Take care of yourself and do what makes you happy every day so you can be the mom and the person you have always wanted to be.

I wish that you remind yourself what a miracle life is, your children, and YOU every day! Thank yourself for all the work you are doing every day.

You can shift your life every day! Be bold and take action. I know you can do it, I know you can.

I am thrilled what you are going to do as the first step. Are you thrilled either? Do it now, no matter how small the action is.

Don't forget:
You are a good mom. You are enough and worthy.

THANK YOU, YOUR MINDFUL MOM

If we really love ourselves,
everything in our lives works.

—*Louise L. Hay*

WIFE. MOM. BOSS.

Inspirations from this book

- Love your little treasures unconditionally, no matter what they did, said, or how "wrong" they behaved. Be mindful of beliefs you plant with your consequences. Your children are extremely sensitive. Be aware of what seeds you plant.

  The most important beliefs you want to cultivate are: *you are enough, you are worthy, and you are lovable*.

- Do the same for yourself. Love yourself unconditionally, no matter what. Use the mantra "I am enough, I am worthy" as often as possible.

- Make time for your loved ones. Spend time with your children. It does not really matter how long; the quality is the most important. Be mindful, in the present moment, and connect fully when you are with your children. Cultivate mindful and present moments and rituals throughout the day.

- Do the same for yourself. Take time for yourself each day.

- Listen, really listen, to your children. Do you really hear what your children try to say? Listen with an open heart. Sit down, drop everything else, look into their eyes, and really care about them. Be mindful and emphatic. Children always feel the difference if the adult really listens or is distracted with something else; you will discover a moistening in the eyes if you are really there.

- Do the same for yourself. Take time to reflect and listen to your inner being, your inner core, your heart, your body, and your thoughts.

- Serve your children and thank yourself.

Keep in mind that every duty you do is a service. You are a goddess because you love them unconditionally, cook, take care, sooth, embrace, clean, wipe tears, dress and undress them, etc. When you do it mindfully, keeping in mind you are doing a great service for your loved ones, you clearly see the purpose of all the little things you do. Besides nourishing your loved ones, you feel stronger, worthy, and more satisfied because you are more aware of your great work. Do not take it for granted. You are doing a great service every day!

- Do the same for yourself. Serve yourself like you do for your loved ones. Create nice moments for yourself daily.
- Give approval and strengthen their self-confidence.
- Notice and catch them when they are good, meaning when they behave well, behave intuitively, generously, sharingly, kindly, and lovingly. Encourage them to practice if anything does not work out. Give approval as often as you can. It will be extremely encouraging for them.
- Do the same for yourself. Praise yourself every day after every task.
- Say how much you love them as often as you can and mean it. Say that you are happy being their mom, that you feel blessed to have such a good and lovable child, that she/he is a huge gift for you from the source (or God/life).
- Do the same with yourself. Appreciate yourself and everything you do and all you are. Like yourself. Be your own best friend.
- Catch every opportunity to thank your little ones. It is a huge uplifter for them because they feel special.
- Do the same with yourself. Say thank you as often as you can for everything. You will discover how soul-nourishing it is.
- See in your child the spark of the divine.
- Do the same for yourself. Imagine what words you would like to hear. You are the best, you are a good mom, you are beautiful, I like you so much, you are amazing, etc. Say the words to yourself as often as you can. Do not wait and expect the words from others. If you need approval and praise from others, it makes you needy. If you praise yourself and give approval to yourself, it makes you strong, and it lifts you up.
- Take care of yourself: Start with a few minutes (three to five minutes) a day and broaden it more and more. Five minutes consistently is better than nothing. Create nice moments for yourself. Seek silence and being with yourself at least a few minutes every day.
- Be aware of your thoughts. They create your feelings. Feelings create your actions.
- Be aware of your language. Instead of saying *I have to/need to/must/should/*

94

shouldn't, say I may, I can, I would like to, this is a chance to, this is a step to.

❧ Cultivate a *gratitude journal/book of appreciations/book of my blessings.*

❧ Don't forget: *You are too blessed to be stressed.*

❧ Do what you are passionate about every day! You will raise your energy and mood and be the best mom.

❧ Never beat up on yourself. Instead, ask, when there is a step back/challenge, *what can I learn from this? What is this teaching me? How can I grow from this? What opportunity does it present to me?*

❧ Release all expectations of your children, yourself, and others. This is a healing process (notice, just reading this sentence feels so freeing).

❧ And finally, to blossom every day, do everything— I mean it like I say it, EVERYTHING!—with fun, enjoyment, creativity, inspiration, and ask always *how can I/we have more fun?* Remind yourself to have fun and enjoy the journey as a parent daily with love and dedication.

This is your worthy life with your worthy children who adore you!

Peace and Freedom

Stop doubting myself

Stop yelling at myself

Stop feeling guilty

Enjoy the present moment

Be aware of your blessings

And feel inner peace flowing into your body

Connect to your breath and yourself

Feel contentment about yourself and the world

Do the things you love and love the things you do

Appreciate all the small things, they aren't small

That's what life is all about

See your children as they truly are:

Little buddhas; mindful; joyous; shining; endlessly beautiful in- and outside; worthy, no matter what; smart; gorgeous; bright; precious; perfect as they are; and so much more.

Unless you become as little children, you cannot enter the Kingdom of God.

— *Matthew 18:3*

Resources

If you would like to dive in deeper, below is a list of some of my favorites books I read and where I got inspired to grow my *Mindful Mom mind-set*. Also, my favorite teachers, I really appreciate, and I am grateful for everything I learned from them.

If you would like the short cut and are too busy, I recommend all the magazines below. Or you can search every author or teacher on YouTube. There, you can discover many interviews, webinars, and guided meditations.

Books
Benson, Herbert and William Proctor. *Relaxation Revolution.*
Books, Cico. *Empowering Mantras for Awesome Women.*
Chopra, Deepak. *The Seven Spiritual Laws for Parents.*
Dispenza, (Dr.) Joe. *Breaking the Habit of Being Yourself.*
Goodard, Neville. *The Power of Awareness.*
Katie, Byron. *Loving What Is: Four Questions That Can Change Your Life.*
Lakhiani, Vishen. *The Code of the Extraordinary Mind.*

Lyubomirsky, Sonja. *The How of Happiness – A Scientific Approach of the Life You Want.*
Murphy, Joseph. *Within You Is the Power.*
Seligman, Martin E. P. *Authentic Happiness.*
Sincero, Jen. *You Are a Badass – How to Stop Doubting Your Greatness and Start Living an Awesome Life.*
Tsabary, Shefali. *The Conscious Parent.*
Verni, Ken A. *Happiness - The Mindful Way.*

Magazines
Breathe: THE MINDFULNESS SPECIAL
Centennial Health: THE POWER OF MINDFULNESS
National Geographic: EVERYDAY MINDFULNESS
Time: MINDFULNESS-THE NEW SCIENCE OF HEALTH AND HAPPINESS
Time: THE NEW MINDFULNESS
Women's Health: THE NEW MINDFULNESS
Yoga Journal: THE POWER OF MINDFULNESS

Online Resources
www.bensonhenryinstitute.org
www.iamenough.com
www.mindvalley.com
www.positiveparentingsolutions.com

Online Seminars/Trainings
PART (Positivity and Relaxation Training, General Hospital, Benson Henry Institute, Massachusetts)
The Science of Well-Being (Yale University by Prof. Dr. Laurie Santos)

Teachings/Webinars
Eckhart Tolle
Esther Hicks
Jon Kabat-Zinn
Louise L. Hay
Marisa Peer
Robert Betz
Veit Lindau
Wayne Dyer
Mindvalley webinars: Dr. Michael Breus, Dr. Shefali Tsabary, Dr. Srikumar Rao, Jon and Missy Butcher, Marisa Peer, Michael Beckwith, Robin Sharma; Vishen Lakhiani

Thanks and blessings to . . .

My biggest appreciation goes to my husband who always believes in me. Who always makes sure I have time for myself and pursuing my passions in my profession, living my dreams and heart's desires. I am so grateful life connected our souls together. Thank you for your unconditional love.

Heartfelt thanks to my gorgeous three boys who gave me so much time, patience, and inspiration to create this book. Every day there are plenty of situations I feel joy and happiness because of them. Because of them, I love being a mom with my whole being.

Thanks to my family: My parents are the reason I am on earth. (We should never forget this fact.) I am so grateful for their love and all the efforts they did to raise us and make us happy. Without my dad, we wouldn't be in Germany, one of the richest countries in the world, with outstanding chances to fulfill your purpose. I am so thankful that he (and my grandma) made this life here possible. I appreciate my mom as my role model who followed fearlessly her passion to become a doctor and has incredibly high willpower. I love to share my passion with her about humans' psyche and about creativity. To my sister, thank you that you always believe in me and my skills, that you always try to connect our lives, although we live far away from each other.

Furthermore, there is this huge supportive social-connecting power coming from my closest friends Svenja, Rosa, Agnes, Anna, Tanja, Yvonne, Stefanie, Kay, Chelsea, Priska, Linda A., Linda Na. and Linda Ne. I feel blessed to have them as my chosen extended family. I know they have my back no matter what. Thanks for being so heartfelt, uplifting, and interested in our life. Thanks for encouraging me about all my *crazy ideas*, supporting me, listening to me, and being happy for us and our happiness and bliss.

Also, I would like to thank my neighbors and friends who helped me in the correction process: Linda, Baltia, Virginia, Lisa, Yvonne, Carol, and Candice and Courtney. I appreciate your worthy time (the biggest gift you can make for someone). It means a lot to me.

Thanks to source/spirit/God who gave me the inspiration, skills, and creativity for this book. I feel inner trust that I am safe, supported, and guided. Thank you for the blessing being a mom and my wonderful life.

Thanks to Xlibris for helping me publish this book.

My last appreciation goes to you—thanks for taking time reading this book. Thanks for letting the ideas and inspirations sink in, growing in self-care and strengthening yourself. This is a huge gift for everyone around you.

You are enough and worthy. You are a good mom.

Printed in the United States
by Baker & Taylor Publisher Services